# FRANZ SCHUBERT

# SYMPHONY No. 5

B♭ major/B-Dur/Si♭ majeur
D 485

Edited by / Herausgegeben von
Richard Clarke

T0084449

## Ernst Eulenburg Ltd

London · Mainz · Madrid · New York · Paris · Prague · Tokyo · Toronto · Zürich

# CONTENTS

# PREFACE

Schubert's formative years as a chorister at the Imperial Court Chapel in Vienna and his subsequent education at the prestigious *Stadtkonvikt* [city seminary] brought him into direct and almost daily contact with the Classical Viennese repertoire centred on the works of Haydn, Mozart and Beethoven. This repertoire was by no means limited to vocal music. In his memoir of the composer published a few months after Schubert's death, his lifelong friend, Josef von Spaun, recalls in close and illuminating detail the young composer's active and daily participation in orchestral music at this time:

[...] the instrumental music at the *Stadtkonvikt* had, by diligent collaboration among the pupils, been brought to a degree of perfection rarely to be found among such young amateurs. Each evening was devoted to the performances of a complete symphony and several overtures, and the young orchestra's forces sufficed for the successful performance of Haydn's, Mozart's and Beethoven's masterpieces. Schubert, scarcely 12 years of age, played second violin and later was placed as leader at the head of the orchestra [...] Above all the glorious symphonies in G minor [No. 40, K550] by Mozart and in D major [No. 2] by Beethoven made the profoundest impression on the young Schubert every time, and even shortly before his death he still spoke of how greatly these compositions had moved and touched his youthful soul.[1]

Spaun (who shared the orchestral second violin desk with Schubert) further informs us that having lost his soprano voice and with it his place as a choirboy, Schubert 'resolved to leave the seminary and also to give up his studies, in order to follow his profession as composer undividedly'.[2]

But this was not to prove an easy endeavour. In 1814 at the age of 17 Schubert trained as a primary schoolteacher and was subsequently employed as an assistant at his father's school, and a full-time career as a schoolmaster seemed likely for in April 1816 he made a late application for the post of Musical Director at the German Normal School in Laibach (now Ljubljana in Slovenia) accompanied by a testimonial from the Court Musical Director Antonio Salieri. In early September, however, he learned that his application had failed. During this 'schoolmaster' period Schubert composed a large number of works in all genres, including opera, and it was during the latter part of this period, during the years 1815–16, that Schubert wrote his symphonies Nos. 2–5.

The sound-world of the Fifth Symphony is determined by its modest instrumentation which (as in Mozart's Symphony No. 40) excludes clarinets, trumpets and drums; a restriction that lends the work a chamber music quality. The opening *Allegro* begins neither with a slow introduction (which had been Schubert's symphonic habit up till now) nor with the immediate statement of the principal theme itself. Instead, Schubert prefaces the principal theme with an elegantly-scored 4-bar chordal progression in the woodwinds with an extended anacrusic scale figure in the violins, which is at once both simple in construction and complex in its structural function. This prefatory chord progression has been compared to the drawing back of a theatrical curtain before the play commences and it is indeed a useful analogy. The structural significance of the 4-bar chordal preface is realized at the opening of the development section (bb118ff) where it forms the basis of a 4-fold modulatory sequence that sets the development in motion. A modified version of the chordal preface heralds the recapitulation (bb171ff) which contains its own formal surprises. Instead of presenting an identical repetition of the

[1] Quotation from the *Österreichisches Bürgerblatt für Verstand, Herz und gute Laune*, Linz, 27 and 30 March and 3 April 1829. Anonymous, but written by Josef von Spaun. Otto Erich Deutsch, *Schubert: A Documentary Biography*, trans. Eric Blom (London, 1946), 865–79
[2] Deutsch, ibid., 867

sonata exposition, Schubert presents the return of the principal theme in the subdominant E flat instead of the orthodox tonic; only after an extended transition is the tonic key restored with the entry of the second theme (b231).

The second movement *Andante con moto* reflects the Mozartian practice of adapting the expressive operatic idiom of accompanied aria to orchestral usage. Schubert sets the contrasting wind and string dialogue within a wide-ranging, elaborate and technically assured modulatory scheme.

In part because of their shared keys, Schubert's Menuetto has often been compared with the corresponding movement from Mozart's 40th Symphony K550. The similarities, however, remain superficial and Schubert's Menuetto does not, for instance, attempt to emulate Mozart's subtle contrapuntal agility. The Trio section is of the pastoral *Ländler* type beginning with a near-exact inversion of the minuet subject.

The sonata-form Finale feels closer to Haydn's symphonic world, particularly with its extended *piano* opening balanced by the *forte* passage beginning at b27 and with the second subject being preceded by a silent upbeat pause (b78). The development section (bb153ff) is based on the opening figure with characteristically adroit Schubertian exploratory modulations. The sonata recapitulation (bb237ff), in contrast to that of the opening movement, reproduces the exposition – apart from the neces-sary changes to the transition – as closely as possible and without the need for a concluding coda.

The reception history of the Fifth Symphony during the 19th-century is extremely modest. Schubert completed the symphony on 3 October 1816 and it was likely performed later that month by an amateur orchestral society that met under the leadership of Otto Hatwig of the Burgtheater Orchestra and in which the composer played the viola. The symphony was not published during Schubert's lifetime, and (as far as is known) remained unplayed for over a quarter of a century when it was given its first public performance on 17 October 1841 at the Josef-städter-Theater in Vienna, under the direction of Michael Leitermayer. The first English performance of the symphony took place at the Crystal Palace, London, on 1 February 1873 conducted by August Manns as part of an extended series of Schubert's complete symphonies, and was the direct result of the investigative efforts of Sir George Grove (founding editor of the famous dictionary) and the composer Sir Arthur Sullivan who visited Vienna together in the autumn of 1867 and located the autographs and MS copies of Symphonies 1–6 among other works. The symphony was first published as late as 1885 as part of the *Critical Complete Edition/Kritische durchgesehene Gesamtausgabe*, edited by Eusebius Mandyczewski and Johannes Brahms.

Richard Clarke

# VORWORT

Schuberts prägende Jahre als Sängerknabe an der Kaiserlichen Hofkapelle in Wien und die sich daran anschließende Ausbildung am renommierten Stadtkonvikt brachten ihn unmittelbar und fast täglich mit dem Repertoire der Wiener Klassik in Berührung, das sich auf die Werke von Haydn, Mozart und Beethoven konzentrierte. Dieses Repertoire beschränkte sich keineswegs auf die Vokalmusik. In seinem Nachruf auf den Komponisten, der einige Monate nach Schuberts Tod veröffentlicht wurde, erinnert Schuberts langjähriger Freund Josef von Spaun sehr ausführlich und aufschlussreich an die zu jener Zeit aktive und tägliche Teilnahme des jungen Komponisten an der Orchestermusik:

Gleichzeitig war die Instrumental-Musik in dem Konvikte durch ein eifriges Zusammenwirken der Zöglinge auf einen Grad der Vollkommenheit gebracht, den man bei so jugendlichen Dilettanten selten finden wird. Der Abend war täglich der Aufführung einer vollständigen Sinfonie und einiger Ouvertüren gewidmet, und die Kräfte des jugendlichen Orchesters reichten hin, die Meisterwerke Haydns, Mozarts und Beethovens auf eine gelungene Weise in Aufführung zu bringen. Der kaum 12jährige Schubert spielte die zweite Violine im Orchester mit. […] und bald wurde der kleine Knabe als Leiter an die Spitze des Orchesters gestellt [...]. Vor allem machten die herrlichen Sinfonien aus [sic!] g-Moll [Nr. 40, KV 550] von Mozart und D [Nr. 2] von Beethoven jedesmal den tiefsten Eindruck auf den jungen Schubert, und noch kurz vor seinem Tode sprach er davon, wie sehr diese Musikstücke sein jugendliches Gemüt ergriffen und gerührt haben.[1]

Spaun (der im Orchester in den zweiten Violinen ein Pult mit Schubert teilte) schreibt außerdem: „Er beschloß daher […], nachdem er überdies seine Sopran-Stimme und mit ihr seine Stelle als Sängerknabe verloren hatte, das Konvikt zu verlassen und auch die Studien aufzugeben, um ungestört der Kunst leben zu können."[2]

Dies war jedoch kein leichtes Unterfangen. Im Jahr 1814, im Alter von 17 Jahren, unterrichtete Schubert an einer Schule und wurde anschließend als Hilfslehrer an der Schule seines Vaters angestellt. Eine hauptberufliche Tätigkeit als Lehrer zeichnete sich ab, doch im April 1816 bewarb er sich – ausgestattet mit einem Empfehlungsschreiben des Hofkapellmeisters Antonio Salieri – um die Stelle als Musikdirektor an der deutschen Schule in Laibach (heute Ljubljana in Slowenien). Anfang September erhielt er jedoch eine Absage. Während dieser Zeit als Lehrer komponierte Schubert eine große Anzahl an Werken aller Gattungen, einschließlich Opern. In der späteren Hälfte dieser Periode, in den Jahren 1815–1816, komponierte Schubert die Sinfonien Nr. 2–5.

Die Klangwelt der Sinfonie Nr. 5 wird durch ihre sparsame Instrumentierung (wie in Mozarts Sinfonie Nr. 40) ohne Klarinetten, Trompeten und Pauken bestimmt; eine Einschränkung, die dem Werk kammermusikalische Eigenschaften verleiht.

Der Eröffnungssatz, Allegro, beginnt weder mit einer langsamen Einleitung (was bis dahin charakteristisch für Schuberts sinfonischen Stil war) noch mit einer sofortigen Einführung des Hauptthemas. Stattdessen leitet Schubert das Hauptthema über vier Takte mit einer elegant instrumentierten akkordischen Steigerung in den Holzbläsern sowie mit einer erweiterten auftaktigen Tonleiterfigur in den Violinen ein. Dies ist gleichsam einfach im Aufbau als auch komplex in der Struktur. Diese einleitende Akkordfortschreitung wurde mit dem Zurückziehen des Theatervorhangs vor Beginn eines Stückes verglichen – und dies ist in der Tat ein passender

---

[1] Josef von Spaun: *Über Schubert*. Spauns Nachruf erschien anonym zwischen dem 27. März und 3. April 1829, in drei Teilen, im *Österreichischen Bürgerblatt für Verstand, Herz und gute Laune*, hrsg. v. Friedrich Eurich in Linz, sowie unter dem Titel „Über Franz Schubert", in: Otto Erich Deutsch, *Schubert. Die Erinnerungen seiner Freunde*, Leipzig 1957, S. 24–25.

[2] Deutsch, ebda., S. 26.

Vergleich. Die strukturelle Bedeutung der 4-taktigen akkordischen Einleitung wird zu Beginn des Durchführungsteils deutlich (Takt 118ff.), wo sie die Grundlage für eine vierfache Modulationsfolge bildet, welche die Durchführung einleitet. Die Reprise (Takt 171ff.), die ihre eigenen formalen Überraschungen beinhaltet, wird durch eine veränderte Version der akkordischen Einleitung angekündigt. Schubert präsentiert keine identische Wiederholung der Exposition, sondern eine Wiederkehr des Hauptthemas in der Subdominante Es, anstelle der üblichen Tonika; erst nach einer erweiterten Überleitung wird die Tonika mit dem Beginn des zweiten Themas (Takt 231) wiederhergestellt.

Der zweite Satz, Andante con moto, spiegelt die Praxis Mozarts wider, die expressive Opernsprache der begleiteten Arie auf den orchestralen Gebrauch zu übertragen. Schubert setzt den kontrastreichen Dialog zwischen Bläsern und Streichern innerhalb eines weitreichenden, raffinierten und technisch überzeugenden Modulationsschemas ein.

Schuberts Menuetto wurde teilweise wegen der gleichen Tonarten mit dem entsprechenden Satz aus Mozarts Sinfonie Nr. 40, KV 550, verglichen. Die Ähnlichkeiten bleiben jedoch oberflächlich; Schuberts Menuetto versucht beispielsweise nicht, Mozarts subtile kontrapunktische Beweglichkeit nachzuahmen. Der Trioteil ist im Stil eines pastoralen Ländlers gehalten, der mit einer fast exakten Umkehrung des Menuett-Themas beginnt.

Das Finale in Sonatenform erinnert mehr an Haydns sinfonische Welt, besonders mit seiner erweiterten Eröffnung im Piano, die durch die in Takt 27 beginnende Passage im Forte ausgeglichen wird, und mit dem zweiten Thema, dem ein Auftakt mit einer Fermate über der Pause (Takt 78) vorangeht. Der Durchführungsteil (Takt 153ff.) basiert auf der Eröffnungsfigur mit den für Schubert charakteristisch geschickten und erfinderischen Modulationen. Die Reprise (Takt 237ff.) gibt im Gegensatz zur Reprise des Eröffnungssatzes die Exposition – ausgenommen der erforderlichen Wechsel zur Überleitung – ziemlich identisch wieder und erfordert keine abschließende Coda.

Die Rezeptionsgeschichte der Sinfonie Nr. 5 während des 19. Jahrhunderts ist äußerst bescheiden. Schubert vollendete die Sinfonie am 3. Oktober 1816. Sie wurde wahrscheinlich einen Monat später von einer Liebhaber-Orchestergesellschaft aufgeführt, die unter der Leitung von Otto Hatwig vom Burgtheater-Orchester zusammenkam und in der der Komponist Viola spielte. Die Sinfonie wurde nicht zu Schuberts Lebzeiten veröffentlicht und (soweit dies bekannt ist) über ein Vierteljahrhundert lang nicht gespielt. Die erste öffentliche Aufführung des Werkes fand schließlich am 17. Oktober 1841 am Josefstädter-Theater in Wien unter der Leitung von Michael Leitermayer statt. Die erste Aufführung der Sinfonie in England fand am 1. Februar 1873 im Crystal Palace in London unter der Leitung von August Manns als Teil einer erweiterten Konzertreihe mit Schuberts gesamten Sinfonien statt. Dies resultierte aus den Forschungstätigkeiten von Sir George Grove (Gründungsherausgeber des berühmten Lexikons) und dem Komponisten Sir Arthur Sullivan, die im Herbst 1867 zusammen Wien besucht hatten und die Autographe und Manuskriptabschriften der Sinfonien Nr. 1–6 zwischen anderen Werken gefunden hatten. Die Erstveröffentlichung der Sinfonie fand erst im Jahr 1885 als Teil der *Kritisch durchgesehenen Gesamtausgabe*, herausgegeben von Eusebius Mandyczewski und Johannes Brahms, statt.

Richard Clarke
Übersetzung: Uta Pastowski

# SYMPHONY No. 5

Franz Schubert
(1797–1828)
D 485

I. **Allegro**

Edited by Richard Clarke
© 2012 Ernst Eulenburg Ltd, London
and Ernst Eulenburg & Co GmbH, Mainz

24

## II. Andante con moto

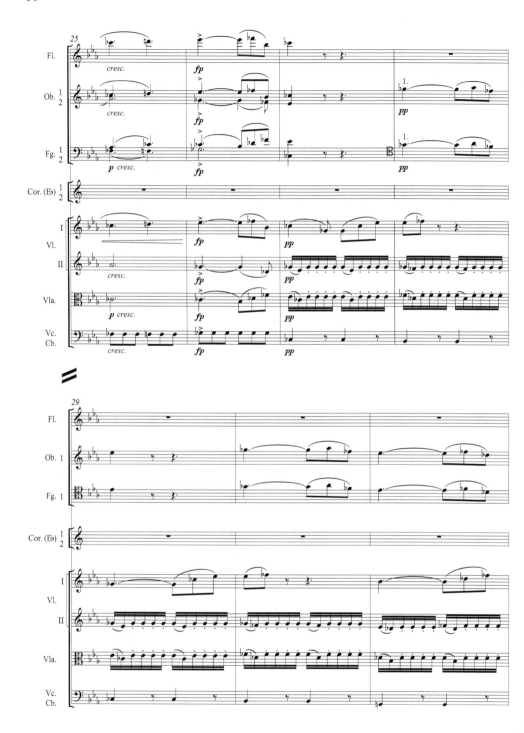

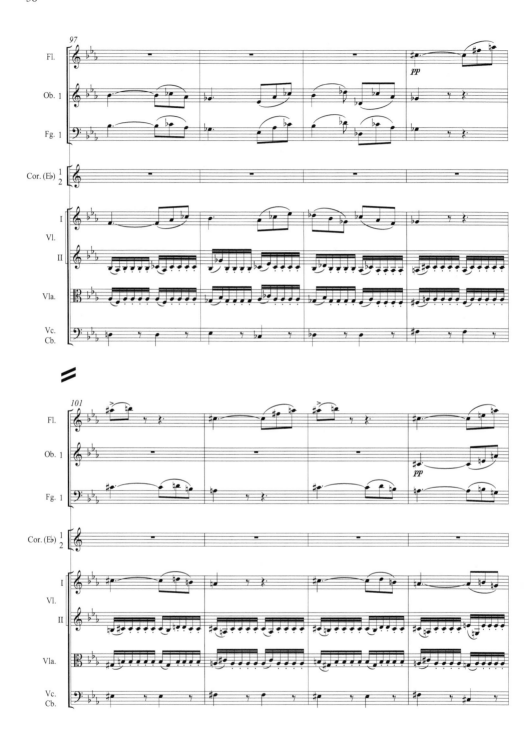

## III. Menuetto

**Allegro molto**

44

48

Trio

Menuetto da capo

# IV. Allegro vivace

54

74